EDINBURGH

THE CLASSIC OLD PHOTOGRAPHS

JAMES McCARROLL

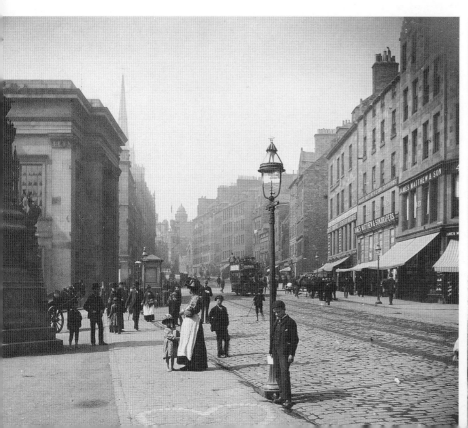

CONTENTS

Front cover | PRINCES STREET, THE SCOTT MONUMENT, THE NATIONAL GALLERY AND EDINBURGH CASTLE, 1897. A wonderful photograph (from the George Washington Wilson collection) that captures the east end of Scotland's most famous thoroughfare towards the end of the Victorian era. Princes Street is, as one would expect, very busy with cabs and brakes plying their trade.

Back cover | EDINBURGH CASTLE FROM GRASSMARKET, 1870s. A stunning photograph, also by Wilson, that shows the full majesty of the castle, and its defensive prowess.

Title page | THE HEART OF MIDLOTHIAN, HIGH STREET, 1883 (*left*). This heart-shaped mosaic, in granite, marks the site of the old tollbooth (demolished 1817), which was not only a centre for the collection of tolls but also served as a town hall and as a notorious prison.

It is mentioned in Scott's novel, *The Heart of Midlothian*, hence the name. Many passers-by spit on the heart, which originally indicated disdain for the prison, but is now said to bring good luck.

ROYAL SCOTTISH ACADEMY, PRINCES STREET, 1911 (*right*). Designed by William Playfair and completed in 1826, this is an imposing Doric temple (Playfair enlarged it in 1831) that never fails to impress. Topped by a huge, 1844 statue of Queen Victoria, dressed as Britannia. Founded as the Scottish Academy, the RSA received its royal charter in 1838, making it the oldest artists' collective in Scotland. Academicians (members) are artists or architects who were born, or now live, in Scotland, elected by their peers. The RSA has an outstanding collection of Scottish art and, in addition, stages exhibitions throughout the year.

This page | PALACE OF HOLYROODHOUSE, 1901 (*see* 27).

INTRODUCTION

In common with most cities Edinburgh has been shaped by geology and geography. The Edinburgh volcano consisted of what we now call Castle Rock and Arthur's Seat. Around 325 million years ago the great volcano erupted, forming excrescences such as Calton hill, then became dormant. During the Ice Age an ice sheet passed over Edinburgh, creating deep hollows where Grassmarket, Cowgate and the Nor' Loch (present-day Princes Street Gardens) are located. The ice also created a crag-and-tail effect, which runs from the castle down the gentle slope of the Royal Mile to Holyrood.

The sheer height of Castle Rock, not to mention the rugged crags on three sides, made it a natural fortress, a fact not lost on our ancestors. Indeed, it is believed that the great rock has been occupied for seven thousand years: first by local tribes, such as the Votadini, then in all likelihood by the Romans, followed by the Angles and finally by the Scots in the middle of the tenth century. As for the name 'Edinburgh' it was first recorded in the seventh century when the rock and its redoubt was known as Din Eidyn, or the 'fort at Edin'.

There were the beginnings of a town here from the eleventh century and it is thought that David I granted a charter to Edinburgh – extending to 143 acres – around 1120. Prosperity was another matter altogether. Constant incursions by the English were an all-too-regular occurrence. The mighty castle, which still dominates the city skyline, was one response to the threat of invasion. But stout defences were essential everywhere and maps produced in the sixteenth century show a compact burgh protected on three sides by the city wall with its five gates, or 'ports' as they were known in Scotland. There was another town to the east, Canongate, but this was an independent burgh with its own charter and quite separate from Edinburgh.

As Edinburgh prospered – helped of course by its proximity to the great port of Leith – it also expanded. To the south, in Cowgate and Grassmarket, a new suburb was born, enhanced by three great religious houses: Blackfriars monastery, the later Greyfriars monastery and the collegiate church of Kirk o' Field. After 1513 these new developments were enclosed by the Flodden wall, a necessary evil after a crushing defeat by the English. The population continued to grow but the Flodden wall constrained the outward expansion of the Old Town for as much as 250 years. When new accommodation was needed Edinburgh had to build upwards instead, resulting in tenements that could be up to fourteen storeys high.

This could not continue indefinitely. The overcrowding became too great. Therefore, in the middle of the eighteenth century plans were put in place to expand to the north, which meant constructing new bridges, roads and the draining of the Nor' loch. This period saw the birth of the New Town, which developed into one of the finest examples of town planning anywhere in the world.

Along with population growth Edinburgh had become yet more important in political terms. The castle, so significant militarily, also served as a royal residence from the eleventh century. The windswept and rather bleak location made it a less than congenial home for Scotland's kings and queens with most electing to live in the palace of Holyroodhouse, which became the official residence of the monarchy in 1503. A parallel development was that the town had become the regular meeting place of the Scots parliament. It was only a matter of time before Edinburgh became the official capital of Scotland.

With the increase in Edinburgh's political significance it was hardly surprising that its intellectual status also grew. Scotland had been at the forefront of providing every child, no matter how humble their birth, with an education and Edinburgh was no exception. The establishment of Edinburgh university in 1583, by James VI, further enhanced the town's status. Along with an institution devoted to higher education and a highly literate populace, Edinburgh could add a great many other advantages: it was home to the civil service, the most important law courts, the established church, the elite of the medical profession, most publishers and printers, and, before 1707, the Scots parliament. This brought with it a huge amount of intellectual capital and in time would make the city the beating heart of what became known as the Scottish Enlightenment.

The word Enlightenment is often associated with the French, with the France of Voltaire, Diderot and Rousseau. Yet the Scottish version does not suffer by comparison. It is no exaggeration to claim that in the eighteenth and early-nineteenth centuries Scotland was at the forefront of new thinking in science, philosophy, medicine and literature, with Edinburgh the epicentre. It was famously said by a visitor that you could 'stand at the

Mercat Cross and, in half an hour, shake fifty men of genius by the hand'. Scientist, inventor and statesman Benjamin Franklin agreed, noting that he had met many 'men of genius' on a visit to the city while his compatriot, Thomas Jefferson, third president of the United States, opined that the 'University of Edinburgh possessed a set of truly great men, Professors of Several Branches of Knowledge, as have ever appeared in any age or country'.

Who were these intellectual giants? David Hume, one of the greatest of all philosophers, was born in Edinburgh and attended the university before producing ground-breaking works, such as *A Treatise of Human Nature* in 1739. Adam Smith, a close friend of Hume, is generally regarded as the father of economics, thanks largely to *The Wealth of Nations*, first published in 1776, and still the most influential economics book of all time. Smith lectured at the university and lived in Canongate for many years. James Hutton, the founder of modern geology, was also born and educated in Edinburgh and was a friend of both Smith and of Joseph Black, the great chemist.

Yet if there is one field in which Edinburgh can claim pre-eminence it is literature. The city of course was the birthplace of Sir Walter Scott (1771–1832), the greatest novelist of the age, educated in the city's schools and at the university before practising law in its courts. Scott more than any other writer invented the historical novel and in works such as *Waverley, Ivanhoe, The Antiquary, Rob Roy* and *The Heart of Midlothian* – most with Scottish themes – he transfixed not only British readers but also lovers of fiction across the world. In 1802, during Scott's lifetime, the *Edinburgh Review* was founded. With its rigorous intellectual standards, it quickly became the most influential periodical in Britain. The *Review* carried articles by the major thinkers of the time, including Carlyle, Hazlitt and Macaulay, and its scope went well beyond literature, embracing history, economics and politics.

Another literary giant born and educated in Edinburgh was Robert Louis Stevenson (1850–94). A scion of the eminent Stevenson family of civil engineers and lighthouse builders, young Robert, like Scott before him, read law at Edinburgh university, and like Scott before him, focused his talents on the novel, penning the masterpieces *Treasure Island, Kidnapped* and *Dr Jekyll and Mr Hyde.* Scott and Stevenson aside the writers associated with the city are legion and a very short list would include Robert Fergusson, J. M. Barrie, Sir Arthur Conan Doyle, Muriel Spark, Alexander McCall Smith, J. K. Rowling and Irvine Welsh. Little wonder that Edinburgh was named the first City of Literature by UNESCO in 2004.

Given its many cultural accomplishments we should perhaps not be surprised that the city is now the home of the world's largest arts festival, the Edinburgh Fringe. As the name implies the Fringe grew out of another event, the Edinburgh International Festival, which was founded in 1947 with the aim of hosting, on an annual basis, the world's leading artists and companies. However, in its first year, eight theatre companies turned up uninvited, and decided to stage their productions on the 'fringe' of the official Festival. A name was coined and a legend was born; the Fringe now puts on more than three thousand shows every August. Complementing the summer arts festivals there is the spectacular Edinburgh military tattoo in which marching bands and musicians from home and abroad put on spectacular shows on the castle esplanade.

Despite its rich history and ancient buildings, Edinburgh, if anything, is becoming yet more important and influential. The population continues to grow, and the city is now home to half a million people. It is a major UK financial centre, second only to London, and one of the biggest in Europe. Then there is the most momentous event of them all: after an absence of three hundred years, the Scots parliament returned to the capital. Abolished by the Act of Union of 1707, which ushered in political union with England, the new parliament convened for the first time on 12 May 1999 in the Church of Scotland's assembly rooms. Since then it has moved to a purpose-built building at the foot of Canongate, across the road from the Palace of Holyroodhouse. Designed by Spanish architect Enric Miralles – and inspired by themes as diverse as the buildings of Antoni Gaudi, the flower paintings of Charles Rennie Mackintosh, upturned boats and the Scottish countryside – it is fair to say that the unique design of this temple of democracy has divided opinion. Yet its presence here is further confirmation of Edinburgh's status as the most important city in Scotland.

OLD TOWN

The mediaeval Old Town consists of the 143 acres sanctioned by David 1 when he founded the burgh of Edinburgh in c.1130. During the Middle Ages, the main thoroughfare, then as now, was High Street. Along with Castlehill, Lawnmarket and Canongate, High Street connected Edinburgh castle with Holyrood palace and by the sixteenth century the whole had become known as the Royal Mile. There were suburbs outside the town walls, Cowgate and Grassmarket, while Canongate itself was an independent burgh until 1856.

As Edinburgh grew so too did the number of houses along the Royal Mile, with nobles and wealthy merchants aspiring to be close to the centre of political power. Many of these properties were built in the back lands, with pends (vaulted passages) leading to hidden closes and tenements. The result was a quite remarkable labyrinth of cobbled streets, narrow alleyways and hidden courtyards. It is our good fortune that much of this historic architecture – along with Georgian additions – has been so well preserved.

The Old Town is always atmospheric with visitors from around the world drawn by its remarkable history and buildings. During the three weeks of the Edinburgh Festival and Fringe – held annually in August – it gets even busier. The Fringe – which has its headquarters in High Street – is the largest arts festival in the world. The statistics are staggering: in 2015 there were fifty thousand performances of more than three thousand shows. Little wonder that, at this time of year, the ancient streets are clogged with performers promoting their shows to potential customers.

The photograph on this page shows the Greyfriars Bobby fountain, which can be found at the junction of George IV bridge and Candlemaker Row. Greyfriars Bobby was a Skye terrier, whose owner, John Gray, was buried in Greyfriars churchyard in 1858. The little dog refused to leave his beloved master's graveside, even in the most inclement weather, keeping watch over it for the next fourteen years, until his own death. This remarkable loyalty endeared Bobby to the people of Edinburgh and he became something of a local celebrity.

1 | GREYFRIARS BOBBY, c.1904

GREYFRIARS' BOBBY, EDINBURGH.   12,186.   G.W.W.

2 & 3 | EDINBURGH CASTLE. The castle is, for many Scots, *the* symbol of the nation. The location helps: atop an extinct volcano, 430 feet above sea level, allowing it to dominate the city's skyline. Down the centuries it has been the scene of many bloody encounters and its military links have endured: as a barracks for Scotland's fighting men and, on the esplanade, as a place for soldiers to parade (*opp. page* c.1900). On this page, in a photograph from 1877, the castle is viewed from Johnston Terrace and it is clear how formidable the natural defences must have been.

EDINBURGH CASTLE FROM JOHNSTON TERRACE 6819 G.W.W.

EDINBURGH CASTLE. FROM JOHNSTON TERRACE. 270. G.W.W.

4 | ESPLANADE, EDINBURGH CASTLE, 1895. Work on the esplanade (a parade ground in front of the castle) began in 1753 and it was widened in 1816. There are many interesting monuments on the north side, including the 78th Highlanders, by Sir Robert Rowand Anderson, an equestrian bronze of Earl Haig by G. E. Wade and Ensign Ewart by William Kininmonth. Today it is perhaps best known as a concert venue, and in particular as the home of Edinburgh's world-famous military tattoo, a spectacular event held annually, in August.

EDINBURGH CASTLE

5 | ROYAL PALACE, CROWN SQUARE, 1912 (*top right*). Begun in the 1430s, this was the sovereign's residence and the repository of the honours of Scotland (crown jewels). It was never a favourite with royalty, who thought it cold and solitary, only taking up residence when there was a military threat. The last monarch to sleep here was Charles I, in 1633.

6 | MONS MEG, n. d. (*bottom left*). The giant cannon was a gift to James II from his niece's husband, Philip, Duke of Burgundy, in 1457. Weighing six tons, it was an extremely powerful, yet cumbersome, weapon of war: it took one hundred men and many horses and oxen a full day to drag it just three miles. Today it is one of the castle's main attractions.

7 | QUEEN'S OWN CAMERON HIGHLANDERS, 1904 (*bottom right*). The castle has served as a barracks for Scotland's regiments for centuries, a trend that has been almost continuous since the mid-seventeenth century.

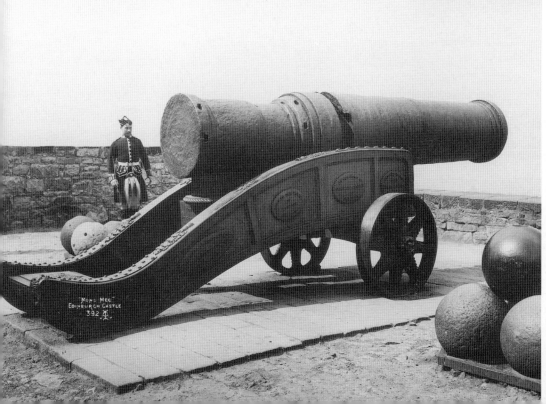

8 | CANNONBALL HOUSE, CASTLEHILL, 1900. Built in the late sixteenth century and named for the cannon ball that is embedded in the west wall. One explanation is that the ball was fired from the castle at Holyrood palace, while Bonnie Prince Charlie was in residence there. This, however, is most likely apocryphal.

9 | TOLBOOTH ST JOHN'S CHURCH, CASTLEHILL, 1910. Partly designed, in the 1830s, by the great ecclesiastical architect, A. W. N. Pugin, this was to be not only a place of worship but also the meeting place of the general assembly of the Church of Scotland. It is one of Scotland's finest Gothic churches and a real Edinburgh landmark. Occupied since 1999 by the Edinburgh International Festival and known as the Hub.

OLD TOWN EDINBURGH. FROM SCOTT MONUMENT. 29.

10 | OLD TOWN FROM SCOTT MONUMENT, 1875. A profile of the Old Town, with Waverley railway station and Waverley bridge in the foreground. North British Railway Company operated the station, which, over the years has been much modified and expanded. As the notice-board shows passengers could catch trains here for Fife, Perth, Dundee and the North as well as local services to Granton, Leith, Portobello, Musselburgh, Dalkeith and Peebles. This is the original Waverley bridge, designed by James Bell and completed in 1873, which was replaced by a later structure in 1896 as part of a major expansion of the station. The spire of St Giles cathedral can be seen in the right background.

11 | MILNE'S COURT, 1910. A redevelopment of existing closes in 1690, by the eponymous Robert Mylne (*sic*), master mason to the Crown of Scotland and a very successful building contractor who carried out the reconstruction of Holyrood palace. Here, he built new blocks on the north and south sides to complement the existing blocks to the east and west. Once family housing, as this photograph shows, it is now student halls of residence.

PARLIAMENT HOUSE SQUARE EDINBURGH. 193. G.W.W.

◀ **12** | LAWNMARKET, 1880. Lawnmarket, a continuation of High Street, runs between the old West Bow (now demolished) and St Giles and developed in the shadow of the castle. The name may be derived from 'land market': that is, the place where merchants from outside the city came to sell their wares, a practice that continued until the late eighteenth century. It would have been a lively scene on market day, with the whole street covered in stalls and canvas booths.

▲ **13** | PARLIAMENT SQUARE, 1877. In 1632 Edinburgh town council, at the request of Charles I, provided a building for the Scottish parliament, the Court of Session and the Privy Council, which came to be known as Parliament House. The present appearance is the result of nineteenth-century modifications by Robert Reid. Although the complex is today concerned with the administration of justice the interior retains the magnificent Parliament hall, once the meeting place for the Scottish parliament. The equestrian statue is of Charles II and was completed in 1685.

WEST FRONT, ST. GILES' CATHEDRAL, EDINBURGH.   3846.   G.W.W.

14 | ST GILES HIGH KIRK/CATHEDRAL, 1904. The church of St Giles has occupied this High Street site since the twelfth century, although most of the exterior we see today dates from the 1820s. The exception is the magnificent crown tower of 1500, a real Old Town landmark. It is said the first action of the Covenanting movement took place in St Giles, when, on 23 July 1637, Jenny Geddes threw her stool at the dean when he read from Laud's liturgy, a text that was anathema to Scots Presbyterians.

15 | MERCAT CROSS, 1910. A well-attended ceremony to mark the death of Edward VII, who had been on the throne since 1901, following the death of his mother, Queen Victoria. The original mercat cross on High Street can be traced as far back as 1365, although it has been moved several times. It was a focus for proclamations and celebrations but also for punishment and the occasional execution. The octagonal cross house (*centre*) is an 1885 copy of the original, complemented by a unicorn finial.

16 | FORMER ROYAL EXCHANGE, 245 HIGH STREET, 1900. The building to the left, behind the pedimented screen, was the royal exchange, conceived by the eminent Scottish architects, siblings John and Robert Adam, whose plans were adapted by contractor John Fergus. It is the only eighteenth-century public building on the Royal Mile and is now occupied by Edinburgh city council. There is an interesting statue by John Steell, *Alexander Taming Bucephalus*, in the courtyard.

17 | JOHN KNOX HOUSE, 45 HIGH STREET, 1865. The great Protestant reformer only lived in this house (*centre right, indicated by sign at top of stairs*) for a short time before his death in 1572. That, however, was enough to save it from demolition during the redevelopment of the 1840s, with the Church of Scotland instrumental in its retention. It was previously occupied by James Mossman, a jeweller and goldsmith, and keeper of the Royal Mint under Mary, Queen of Scots. Mossman remained loyal to Mary and for his pains was executed at the Mercat Cross.

G. McKAY
RNER & BOWLING·GREEN·BOWL·MAKER

9.   JOHN KNOX'S HOUSE. CANONGATE.

CANONGATE, EDINBURGH.   10,558.   G.W.W.

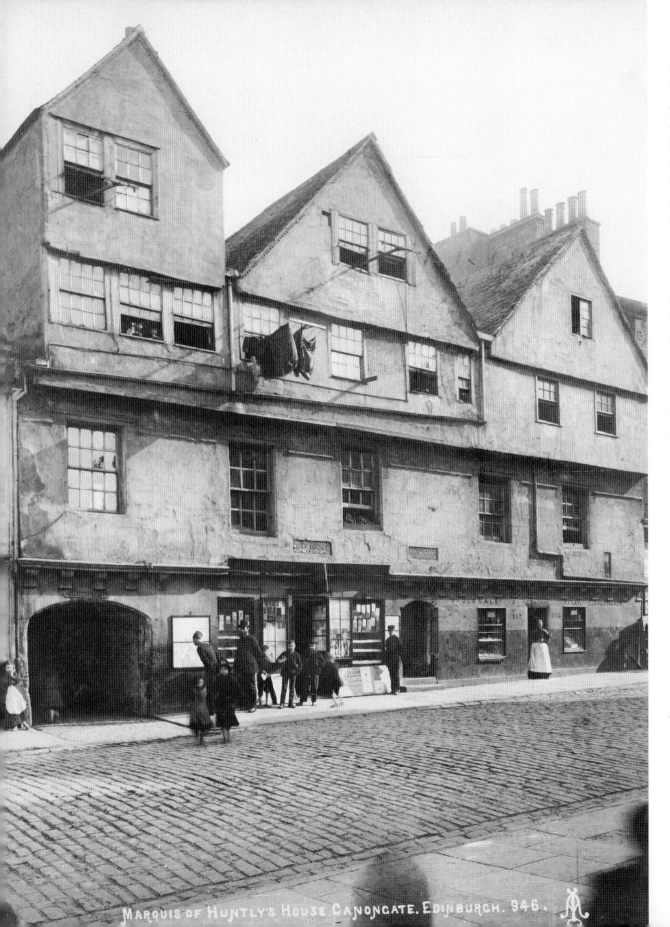

MARQUIS OF HUNTLY'S HOUSE CANONGATE. EDINBURGH. 946.

18 | ALLAN RAMSAY'S HOUSE, 153 HIGH STREET, 1900 (*overleaf*). Ramsay arrived in Edinburgh in 1700 to be apprenticed as a wigmaker. Literature, however, soon took over and he established a storied reputation as poet, dramatist, editor, theatrical impresario and auctioneer. Ramsay's greatest success was his *The Gentle Shepherd*, a drama centring on rustic life. In these premises in High Street, he also set up Scotland's first circulating library. The house was demolished.

19 | CANONGATE, 1904 (*previous page*). The name derives from 'Canon's gait', which was the walk taken by the Augustine monks of Holyrood between their abbey and the walled city of Edinburgh. A town grew up around the abbey and the royal palace, and, in 1143, David I granted a charter, creating the burgh of Canongate. It would remain a proud independent burgh until 1856, when it was incorporated into the city of Edinburgh.

20 | HUNTLY HOUSE, 142 CANONGATE, 1880 (*this page*). These houses date from the sixteenth century, although the only connection to the aristocratic Gordon family of Huntly is that the Duchess of Gordon had a flat here in the mid-eighteenth century. Also known as the 'speaking house' because of the Latin mottoes on the front wall. Now part of the Museum of Edinburgh. Walk through the pend into Bakehouse Close to see the seventeenth-century façade of Acheson house.

21 | TOLBOOTH, 163 CANONGATE, 1900 (*opp. page*). Built in 1591 at the behest of Sir Lewis Bellenden, the historic tolbooth is the oldest surviving building in Canongate. As the name suggests tolls were collected here but it also incorporated the council chamber, which was reached by the external stairs, while prisoners were held in an area below the stairs. The clock dates from 1884. The kilted soldiers – who presumably were returning to their barracks in Edinburgh castle – seem to have been a source of entertainment for local children.

22 | CANONGATE KIRK, 153 CANONGATE,
1900. Built 1688–91 after James VII converted the
parish church of Canongate – which was then
within Holyrood abbey – for use by the Order of
the Thistle. Striking symmetrical design in the
Dutch style by James Smith. Many notables are
buried in the churchyard, including father of
economics Adam Smith and poet Robert Fergusson.

23 | ABBEY SANCTUARY, 1890. Holyrood abbey offered sanctuary to people trying to evade their creditors, whose sanctions against those who owed them money included imprisonment or extreme violence, or indeed both. These unfortunates could apply to the abbot to extend their initial twenty-four-hour protected status for an indefinite period. Such 'tenants' were eventually accommodated in houses built in the vicinity of the abbey. The law changed in the 1880s, meaning that debtors no longer faced prison, and as a result the houses of the abbey sanctuary became businesses, including the Abbey tavern shown here.

24 | ST MARGARET'S LOCH AND ST ANTHONY'S CHAPEL, HOLYROOD PARK (*top left*). The loch, about a third of a mile from Holyrood palace, is man-made and was once a boating pond. Perched on a crag sits St Anthony's, a mediaeval ruin. **25 | MORAY HOUSE, 174 CANONGATE, 190.** (*bottom left*). Built c.1625, this is the finest surviving aristocratic mansion in the O Town. It has a notable place in history: in the early eighteenth century, the Earl Seafield, the Lord Chancellor, was tenant and during his residency the 1707 Trea of Union between Scotland and England was signed. To ensure the deed was dor as discreetly as possible, the signing ceremony took place in the pavilion at the bottom of the garden. **26 | KING JAMES V TOWERS, PALACE OF HOLYROODHOUSE** (*top right*). James IV practically rebuilt the palace in anticipation of his marriage to Margaret Tudor, but his son, James V, was also active, constructing a tower on the north-west side with new royal apartments.

HOLYROOD PALACE & ARTHUR SEAT

27 | PALACE OF HOLYROODHOUSE, 1877. The palace is the official residence of the monarch in Scotland, and, annually, in late June, the Queen carries out a wide range of official engagements, including investitures and hosting a garden party for eight thousand guests. The palace evolved from the royal guest house attached to Holyrood abbey (*far left*), which was founded by David I in 1128. By the fifteenth century Holyrood was firmly established as the pre-eminent royal residence, a status confirmed by James IV, whose rebuilding work made it a palace fit for Scottish kings.

28 | WEST BOW, 1878 (*opp. page*). Connecting Lawnmarket to Grassmarket, West Bow contained many ancient, usually timber-fronted, houses, many owned by prominent citizens. Until the nineteenth century it was one of the most important streets in the city although as a narrow, precipitous, z-shaped street it was very hard for carriages to negotiate. The buildings shown here – including Bowhead house on the corner – survived the 1827 Improvement Act but were later demolished.

29 | VICTORIA STREET (*top right*). There is no definite date for this photograph but it is probably 1880s or 1890s. Dating from the 1840s Victoria Street has some of the city's most attractive structures including the arcaded shopfronts with pedestrian terrace above.

30 | GAELIC CHURCH, NORTH COLLEGE STREET, 1871 (*bottom left*). This church, now demolished, was situated at the junction with College Wynd. North College Street was originally part of the Kirk o' Field Wynd but in 1871 became part of Chambers Street. The official-looking notice on the wall concerns the Edinburgh Improvement Act of 1867 and the redevelopment of the area.

31 | CHAMBERS STREET, 1913 (*bottom right*). The large, Renaissance-style building on the right is the National Museum of Scotland (formerly the Royal Scottish Museum), built between 1861 and 1889 to the plans of Captain Francis Fowke. Worth seeing for the marvellous great hall alone, a huge cast-iron-and-glass space with glazed roof and tiers of balconies.

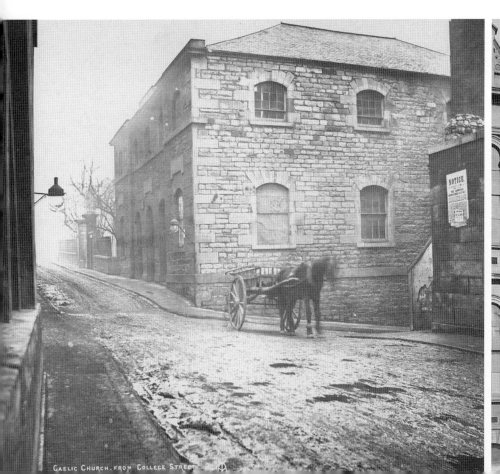

GAELIC CHURCH. FROM COLLEGE STREET.

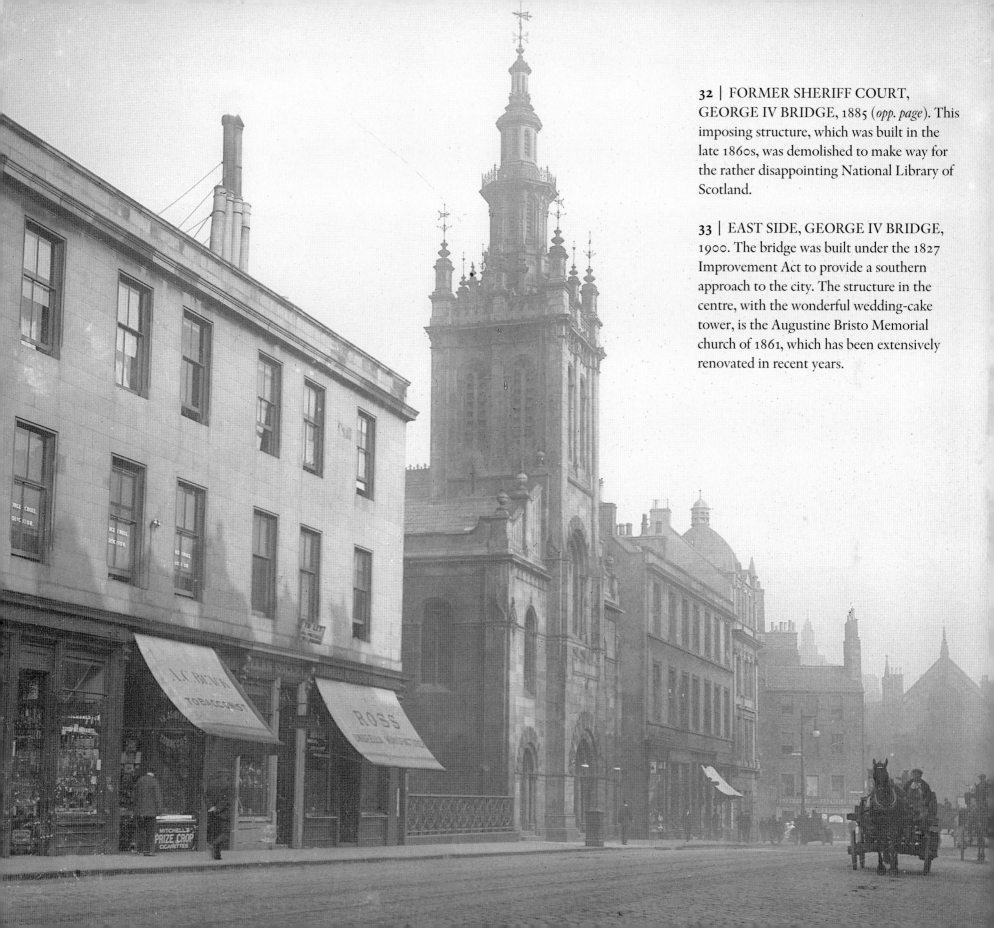

32 | FORMER SHERIFF COURT, GEORGE IV BRIDGE, 1885 (*opp. page*). This imposing structure, which was built in the late 1860s, was demolished to make way for the rather disappointing National Library of Scotland.

33 | EAST SIDE, GEORGE IV BRIDGE, 1900. The bridge was built under the 1827 Improvement Act to provide a southern approach to the city. The structure in the centre, with the wonderful wedding-cake tower, is the Augustine Bristo Memorial church of 1861, which has been extensively renovated in recent years.

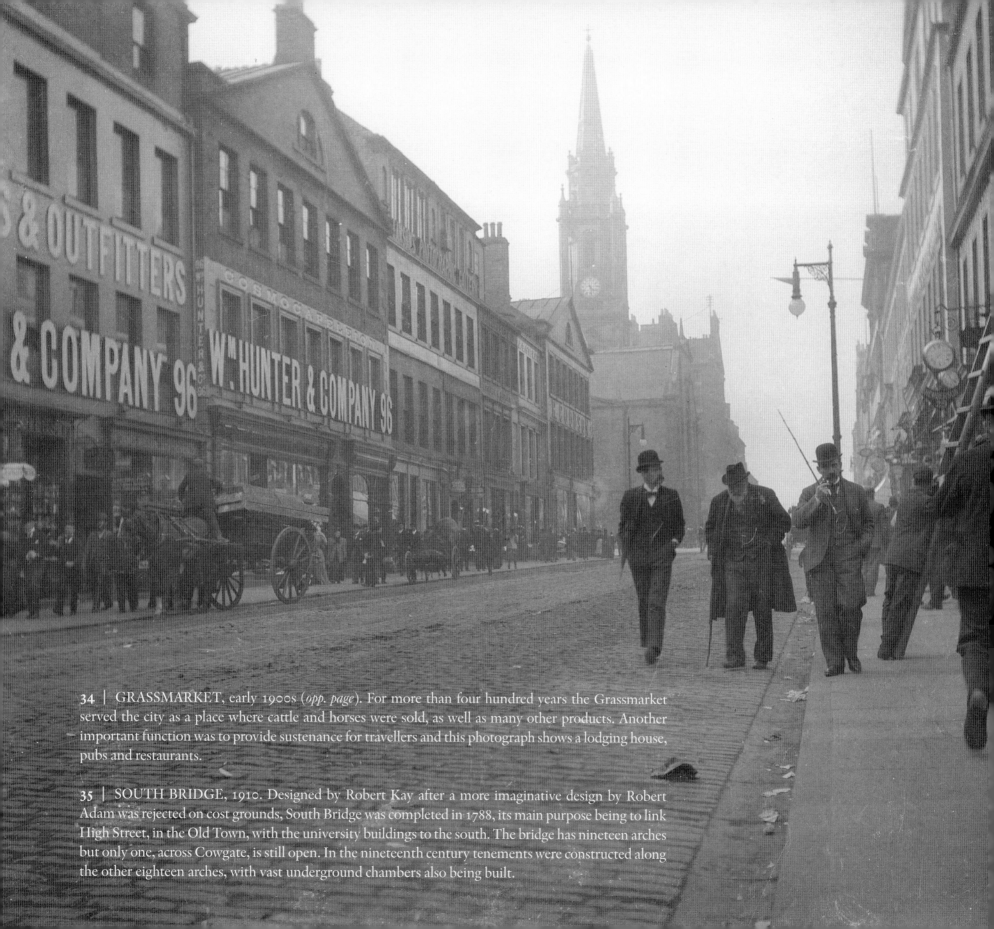

34 | GRASSMARKET, early 1900s (*opp. page*). For more than four hundred years the Grassmarket served the city as a place where cattle and horses were sold, as well as many other products. Another important function was to provide sustenance for travellers and this photograph shows a lodging house, pubs and restaurants.

35 | SOUTH BRIDGE, 1910. Designed by Robert Kay after a more imaginative design by Robert Adam was rejected on cost grounds, South Bridge was completed in 1788, its main purpose being to link High Street, in the Old Town, with the university buildings to the south. The bridge has nineteen arches but only one, across Cowgate, is still open. In the nineteenth century tenements were constructed along the other eighteen arches, with vast underground chambers also being built.

36 & 37 | COWGATE, 1871 and 1900. Another Old Town street whose name derives from its market-day function – 'gate' being a synonym in Scots for way or road – so this was the route along which cows and other livestock would be driven. First recorded as early as 1335 'Cowgait' was once one of the most affluent areas in Edinburgh, described in 1592 as the place 'where the nobility and chief men of the city reside'. Among the aristocratic mansions was one belonging to Thomas Hamilton (1563–1637), Earl of Haddington, who, as president of the Court of Session, Lord Privy Seal and Secretary of State for Scotland, was one of the most influential men in the land. A favourite of James VI, Hamilton was nicknamed by the King, 'Tam o' the Cougait'. However, waves of redevelopment – that included the formation of George IV and South bridges – meant that by the eighteenth century much of its distinctive architecture had been lost. Slums, many of which housed waves of immigrants from Ireland, replaced the old house of the gentry. These photographs of 1871 (*this page*) and 1900 (*opp. page*) give us a fascinating insight into life in Victorian Scotland for the poor.

38 | CARDINAL BEATON'S HOUSE, COWGATE, 1868. David Beaton was one of the most influential Scots of the sixteenth century. Appointed Archbishop of St Andrew's, he would become Scotland's last pre-Reformation cardinal, in 1538. Beaton also wielded considerable political power as ambassador to France and chancellor. Scotland was in turmoil, on the cusp of the Reformation, and Beaton persecuted Protestants with great vigour. It was a policy that would lead to his brutal assassination, in St Andrew's castle, in 1546. His once-splendid palace, with hexagonal tower, became a shop and then slum dwellings for the poor, before being demolished in 1874.

39 | ST MARY'S STREET, early 1900s. Created by the Improvement Act of 1867, the street was formed by the widening of St Mary's Wynd, which had become a notorious slum. As we see, the businesses here include a fruit-and-confections shop, James Hutchinson registered plumber, Rafferty's clothes and the Fish Supper rooms.

40 | HORSE WYND, EAST SIDE,
1871. There are at least four Horse
Wynds recorded in Edinburgh: in
Bristo, Canongate, Leith, and here, the
Cowgate version, which has now been
subsumed by Guthrie, Chambers and
West College streets. These grim-
looking slums were documented by the
photographer, Archibald Burns, prior
to their demolition. The buildings had
already been cleared, hence the removal
sign on the left.

New Town

By the mid-eighteenth century the Old Town was becoming increasingly overcrowded and run down. It was considered an inferior place for the Scottish aristocracy to reside, forcing them, it was thought, to move to more agreeable surroundings in London. The need for change was underlined in 1751 when a tenement collapsed and a subsequent survey of Old Town buildings revealed widespread instability and fire risks. A report by Sir Gilbert Elliott of Minto was published in 1752, in which he argued that radical measures were urgently required if Edinburgh was to remain the principal city of 'North Britain'.

The city fathers – with Lord Provost George Drummond the driving force – decided that a new suburb to the north should be built. A design competition was announced, and, in 1766, it was won by James Craig. The plans formulated by Craig led to what is known as the first New Town, with George Street at its heart. Building began in 1767, but financial problems meant that progress was far from smooth and it was not until 1820 that work was completed. Further, contiguous New Towns followed, a process that took until 1850. The result, it is generally agreed, is one of Europe's finest neoclassical *arrondissements* and the world's largest planned city development. With some justification the New Town has UNESCO world-heritage status.

However, as to the aim of bringing the Scottish aristocracy back from London there is little evidence of success. Perhaps the main effect was to drive the academic, professional and business classes out of the Old Town and into the elegant apartments of such as Moray Place and Great King Street. Where the Old Town had been a social melting pot Edinburgh was now stratified in class terms, with the working and artisan classes left behind as the wealthy moved north.

The photograph here shows the Sir Walter Scott monument in 1890. Honouring Scotland's greatest novelist, it was designed by George Kemp and completed in 1846 at a cost of £15,000. At a height of two hundred feet the Gothic shrine towers above Princes Street and depicts Scott seated, next to his deerhound Maida.

41 | SCOTT MONUMENT, 1890.

EDINBURGH·FROM·THE·CASTLE, 1118. C.W.W

EDINBURGH. FROM. THE. CASTLE, 1118. C.W.W.

42 | EDINBURGH FROM THE CASTLE, 1877. A stunning panorama across Princes Street and its gardens. The railway tunnel servicing Waverley station is in the right foreground, while in the centre we have the Royal Scottish Academy, the National Gallery, and, behind them, the Scott monument. On Princes Street there are shops, horse-drawn vehicles and pedestrians clearly visible. The tall steeple (*background, left*) belongs to St Andrew's and St George's parish church on George Street while the obelisk (*background, centre*) is topped by a statue of Lord Melville.

43 | ROSS BANDSTAND, PRINCES STREET GARDENS, 1900. This fine bandstand was gifted to the city and judging by the number of spectators it appears to have been a popular venue for alfresco music, especially on fine summery days like this. It survived until the 1930s.

44 & 45 | PRINCES STREET: LOOKING WEST TOWARDS NATIONAL GALLERY AND EDINBURGH CASTLE, n. d. (*opp. page*) and **WEST FROM ROYAL SCOTTISH ACADEMY**, 1904 (*this page*). Undoubtedly Scotland's best-known thoroughfare, Princes Street was part of James Craig's first New Town. For the most part it has been built up on one side only (to the north), with the extensive gardens on the south an attractive open space in the heart of the city. The decision not to develop both sides (enshrined in law after several legal battles) has also facilitated spectacular views of the Old Town and Edinburgh castle.

46 & 47 | PRINCES STREET LOOKING EAST, 1875 (*opp. page*) and PRINCES STREET LOOKING EAST, c.1910 (*this page*). Taken thirty-five years apart these photographs show how the rapid advance of new technologies changed the capital, with horse-drawn cabs being replaced by motor vehicles and electric trams. The older image is truly fascinating, taking in not only the Scott Monument (*left*) but also North Bridge and Waverley station (*centre*), and the Old Town (*right*). The newer photograph is equally interesting. Looking east, from right to left, we see the Royal Scottish Academy, the Scott monument, the Balmoral (at that time the North British) hotel and Calton hill.

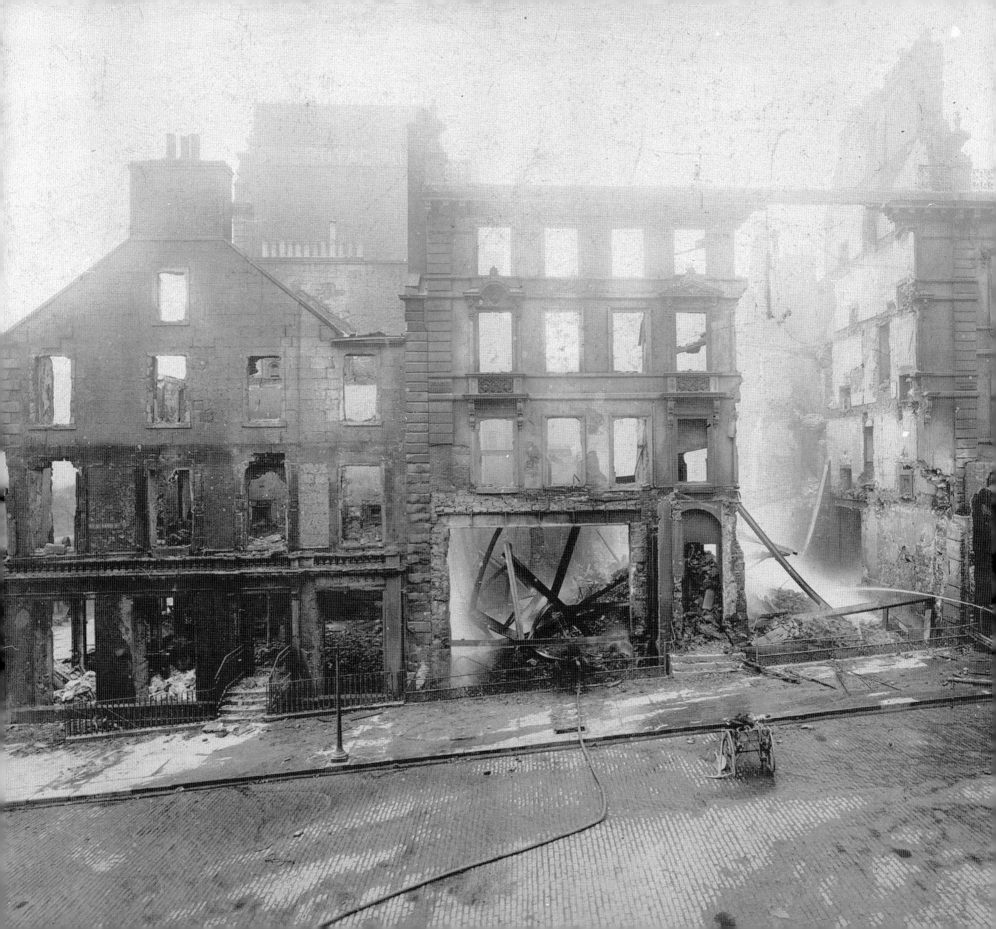

48 & 49 | JENNER'S DEPARTMENT STORE, 48 PRINCES STREET, 1892 and 1895. Charles Jenner started trading on Princes Street in 1838 with partner Charles Kennington. Thanks to their business acumen the Kennington and Jenner department store flourished, enabling it to buy up several neighbouring shops. However, the original shop was destroyed by fire in 1892 (*opp. page*). Undaunted, Jenner set about creating new premises – to include every modern convenience including hydraulic lifts and air conditioning – and the store reopened in 1895. The splendidly opulent exterior, by W. Hamilton Beattie, (*this page*) features magnificent caryatids (female figures), designed to emphasise that women customers were the bedrock of the business. Sadly, Charles Jenner died in 1893 and never got to see his impressive new emporium.

THE BUSINESS OF PRINCES STREET

50 | ROBERT MAULE'S DEPARTMENT STORE (*top left*). Maule's was still a thriving family-run concern in 1902, famed not just for its drapery but also for its electric lift and tearoom. It became *the* place to rendezvous: 'meet me at Maule's' you would tell your friends. Sadly, this fine emporium had disappeared by the 1930s. **51** | PRINCES STREET AND HANOVER STREET, 1900s (*bottom left*). Smartly dressed ladies and gentlemen are taking advantage of the wide selection of Princes Street emporia under the watchful eye of a police constable. **52** | OLD WAVERLEY HOTEL, 1905 (*bottom right*). The Waverley, in the heart of the city, is still operating as a hotel, as is its Cranston's restaurant. The building itself, designed by architect John Armstrong, dates from 1883, and has six storeys plus two in the mansard roof.

53 | PRINCES STREET, WEST END, 1897 (*opp. page*). Edinburgh was still clearly reliant on the noble horse for its transportation needs. Although cable trams were introduced to the city in 1888, the horse-drawn tram seen here was one of a fleet that would not be completely displaced until 1907. The building on the right is St John's church, designed in the Gothic style by William Burn and completed in 1818, with later extensions. Burn's interior is considered by many as a masterpiece.

PRINCES ST. EDINBURGH. FROM WATERLOO PLACE. 2632 GWW.

◀ **54** | WAVERLEY STATION AND CALTON HILL, 1892. The east end of the station was a major depot for coal deliveries. Above it, looms the bulk of the now-demolished Calton jail (*right*) while further up there are the spectacular monuments of Calton hill. The tall, thin column (*background, left*) is a monument to Thomas Muir of Huntershill and the other political martyrs who campaigned for democracy in the 1790s. Muir, who was himself an advocate, was tried in the High Court and sentenced to fourteen years in Botany Bay.

▲ **55** | WATERLOO PLACE LOOKING TOWARDS PRINCES STREET, 1890s. Many architectural historians aver that Robert Adam's Register house (*right*), which opened in the late 1780s, is the finest classical building in the city. It was the first purpose-built repository for public records in Britain and is said to be the oldest archive building in the world still being used for its original purpose. The statue in front of Register house is of the Duke of Wellington, in heroic pose. It was designed by Sir John Steell and completed in 1852. The range of offices and shops on the left would later be demolished and replaced by the North British hotel.

56 | LORD HIGH COMMISSIONER'S PROCESSION, NORTH BRIDGE, 1884. The Lord High Commissioner is the sovereign's personal representative to the general assembly of the Church of Scotland, which meets in Edinburgh every May. Such is the symbolic importance of the role that, during assembly week, the High Commissioner takes precedence after the Queen and the Duke of Edinburgh and before the rest of the royal family. The large crowds here clearly indicate the central importance of the Kirk and organised religion to Victorian Scotland. On the right are passengers and trains at Waverley station.

57 | NORTH BRIDGE AT JUNCTION WITH WATERLOO PLACE AND PRINCES STREET, early 1890s. The original North Bridge dates from 1772 and was the first step in the making of the New Town, providing access from the Old Town. The bridge was widened in the 1870s by the Stevensons and then replaced completely in 1897. This photograph also predates the giant North British hotel, with accommodation in those days being provided by the nicely proportioned but altogether more modest Bridge hotel.

WATERLOO PLACE, EDINBURGH. 2366. G.W.W.

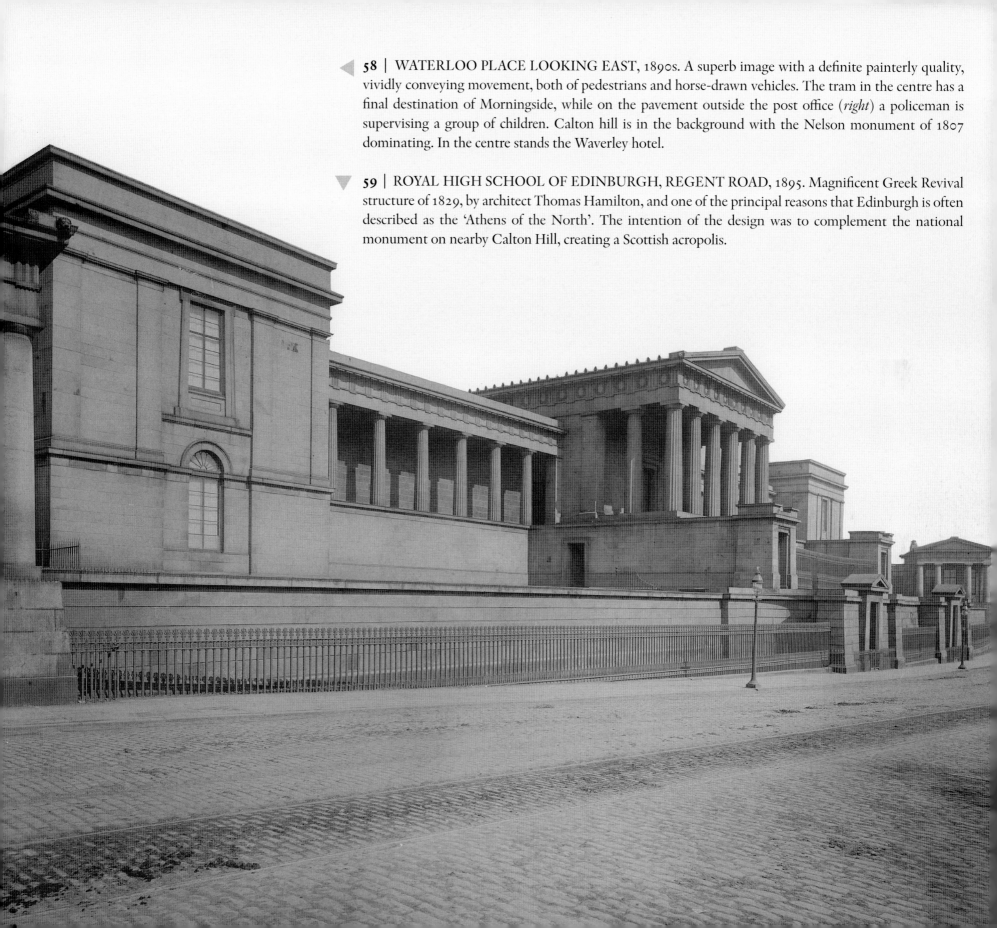

◀ **58** | WATERLOO PLACE LOOKING EAST, 1890s. A superb image with a definite painterly quality, vividly conveying movement, both of pedestrians and horse-drawn vehicles. The tram in the centre has a final destination of Morningside, while on the pavement outside the post office (*right*) a policeman is supervising a group of children. Calton hill is in the background with the Nelson monument of 1807 dominating. In the centre stands the Waverley hotel.

▼ **59** | ROYAL HIGH SCHOOL OF EDINBURGH, REGENT ROAD, 1895. Magnificent Greek Revival structure of 1829, by architect Thomas Hamilton, and one of the principal reasons that Edinburgh is often described as the 'Athens of the North'. The intention of the design was to complement the national monument on nearby Calton Hill, creating a Scottish acropolis.

EDINBURGH. FROM THE CALTON HILL. 33. G.W.W.

60 | EDINBURGH FROM CALTON HILL, 1877 (*opp. page*). A panoramic view that takes in Edinburgh castle, the national gallery, the Scott monument, and, (*centre foreground*) the former Calton jail, where executions in the prison yard could be observed by spectators standing on the hill.

61 | BURNS MONUMENT, CALTON HILL, 1890. A fine tribute to Scotland's national bard, designed by Thomas Hamilton and completed in 1830.

62 | CITY OBSERVATORY, CALTON HILL, 1878. Located on the west summit of Calton hill, the observatory is a classical building of 1812 with four porticoes and central dome, designed by William H. Playfair for the Astronomical Institute. The president of the institute, Professor John Playfair, was an uncle of the architect and his nephew later honoured him with an imposing cenotaph in the shape of the adjacent Playfair monument (*right*). In addition to stargazing the observatory had a secondary but important function, that of providing Edinburgh and Leith with accurate time. Neglected in recent years the building is now being extensively refurbished.

63 | KING EDWARD VII AND QUEEN ALEXANDRA VISIT EDINBURGH, MAY 1903.
Watched by a huge crowd, their majesties cross North Bridge and turn right into Waterloo Place.
Edward VII was born in 1841, the eldest son of Queen Victoria and Prince Albert, but did not succeed
to the throne until 1901, when he was close to sixty. Despite the misgivings of his parents – who
despaired at his laziness, fast lifestyle and raffish tastes – 'Bertie' was a popular and dutiful king who
had a genuine interest in defence and foreign affairs. Perhaps his greatest asset was Alexandra (of
Denmark), a dignified and wise queen.

64 | ST MARY'S CATHEDRAL, PALMERSTON PLACE, 1890. This photograph predates the 1913–17 construction of the twin spires that face Palmerston Place. Based on plans by the great English architect, Sir George Gilbert Scott, the cathedral was constructed between 1874 and 1917, thanks to a legacy from the Walker sisters, Barbara and Mary, heirs to the fortune of Sir Patrick Walker, a prominent Edinburgh property developer. St Mary's design was inspired by the Gothic churches and abbeys of mediaeval Scotland. The huge central tower and spire – which weigh five thousand tons – can be seen for miles.

65 | HOPE STREET, 1897. A marvellous view of the west end of Princes Street at a junction with Hope Street, Lothian Road and Rutland Place with (*from left to right*) the former Robert Maule & Son department store, St John's church, St Cuthbert's church and, in the distance, Edinburgh castle. Note the unusual clock and the distinctly non-utilitarian street lighting.

66 | CHARLOTTE SQUARE FROM PRINCES STREET, c.1900. On the right is the Osborne hotel, which would later become Maule's department store. The impressive domed building on the left is West Register house, an 1814 design by Robert Reid, but based heavily on a plan by Robert Adam, whose scheme of portico, dome and flanking pavilions was retained if in a simpler and more economical fashion. It was originally St George's church but after the Second World War the congregation declined and the building deteriorated. It was taken over by the National Archives of Scotland in the 1960s and now stores records from the courts and government departments.

67 | CASTLE STREET LOOKING SOUTH FROM GEORGE STREET, c.1900. Sir Walter Scott himself lived at 39 Castle Street for more than two decades, from 1802–26, and as a man fascinated by Scottish history we can be sure he would have appreciated the fine view of the castle.

68 & 69 │ CHARLOTTE SQUARE, 1890 AND CHARLOTTE SQUARE GARDENS, 1900. As Pevsner notes 'Charlotte Square is the grand finale of the first New Town, the last section to be built.' The man who conceived it was arguably Scotland's greatest architect, Robert Adam, who had been given a brief to create something elegant yet simple. He died in 1792 but work went ahead and the square (*opp. page*) was completed by 1820. Today it is home to financiers, national organisations and Scotland's first minister, whose official residence is Bute house, 6 Charlotte Square. The gardens (*this page*) were laid out in 1808 and behind them, topped by the wonderful dome, is West Register house, originally St George's church (*see 66* for details). The statue the two ladies are admiring is of Albert, Prince Consort and husband of Queen Victoria, designed by Sir John Steell.

GEORGE ST. EDINBURGH. 184 G.W.W.

70 & 71 | GEORGE STREET.
Linking Charlotte Square in the west and St Andrew Square in the east, George Street is the main axis of the first New Town, its most elegant thoroughfare and replete with quite outstanding architecture. The statue in the centre of the facing page – at the intersection with Hanover Street – is of the king best remembered for his often scandalous and always extravagant lifestyle: George IV (1762–1830). Francis Chantrey's bronze of 1831 commemorates his historic visit to Edinburgh in 1822, the first by a British monarch to Scotland for 171 years. There was considerable pomp and circumstance, brilliantly choreographed by Sir Walter Scott. It included a gathering of the clans, which would help to make the wearing of tartan fashionable for lowland Scots. Turning to this page we see 26 George Street, the Commercial Union Insurance building of 1909 by J. M. Dick Peddie, with domed corner, topped by a statue of Prudence by Percy Portsmouth. The photographs are from 1877 and 1909.

ROYAL COLLEGE OF PHYSICIANS. EDINBURGH. 417.

72 | ROYAL COLLEGE OF PHYSICIANS BUILDING, 9 QUEEN STREET, 1880. In the magisterial Pevsner series of architectural guides, the Royal College is described as 'a neo-classical masterpiece' and it is hard to argue with that assessment. Designed by Thomas Hamilton and completed in 1844, the simple, symmetrical style with statues (including one of Hippocrates) is highly effective.

73 | SCOTTISH NATIONAL PORTRAIT GALLERY, 1 QUEEN STREET, 1895. The gallery was a gift to the Scottish nation from J. R. Findlay, owner of *The Scotsman* newspaper. Designed by Sir Robert Rowand Anderson in the Venetian style, and built in red sandstone from Dumfries-shire, it opened in 1889 and was the world's first purpose-built portrait gallery. Many of the people who shaped Scotland have their portraits hung here including Mary, Queen of Scots, Bonnie Prince Charlie, Robert Burns and Sir Walter Scott.

ROYAL INSTITUTION FROM HANOVER ST. EDINBURGH. 3074. G.W.W.

ROYAL INSTITUTION FROM HANOVER ST. EDINBURGH. 3074. G.W.W.

UNIVERSITY QUARTER

Edinburgh University is one of the finest educational establishments in Britain, founded in 1583 after being granted a charter by James VI. Starting with just eighty students it now has 23,000 undergraduates, 12,000 postgraduates and annual income of £800 million. As one might expect its graduates and faculty have been awarded a large number of prestigious awards for academic excellence including many Nobel prizes, the most recent, for physics, going to Professor Peter Higgs for his work in predicting the Higgs boson, which explains how fundamental particles acquire mass. The list of alumni is stellar and includes Sir Walter Scott, James Boswell, Robert Adam, David Hume, Robert Louis Stevenson, Thomas Carlyle, J. M. Barrie, Sir Arthur Conan Doyle, Alexander Graham Bell and three British prime ministers.

As the university has grown so too has its estate. The Robert Adam-designed old college on South bridge is without doubt the jewel in the crown but there are many other buildings of interest, as the photographs on the following pages illustrate. Sadly, for some at least, the Royal Infirmary of Edinburgh on Lauriston Place – which had close ties to the university's medical faculty – has been replaced. However, the bulk of the building will survive the extensive redevelopment of the site, with the university acquiring the old surgical block, which it has pledged sensitively to restore. Designed by David Bryce and completed in 1879 the RIE has an imposing entrance tower and a number of striking turrets. It was at the forefront of Victorian hospital practice, with an open layout approved by Florence Nightingale herself. However, a hospital capable of meeting modern medical standards was required and so, in 2003, the new royal infirmary opened its doors in Little France. On this page we see the medical school of 1888 by Sir Robert Rowand Anderson, photographed in 1900.

74 | HANOVER STREET, LOOKING TOWARDS ROYAL SCOTTISH ACADEMY, 1904.
(*opp. page – see Contents for RSA details*)

75 | MEDICAL SCHOOL, LAURISTON PLACE, 1900.

76 | OLD COLLEGE QUADRANGLE, UNIVERSITY OF EDINBURGH, and, **77** | OLD COLLEGE FROM NICOLSON STREET, both 1900. With an exterior by Robert Adam and interiors by William Playfair, the old college (as it is now referred to) was almost guaranteed to be an architectural masterpiece and so it turned out. Work stated in 1789 and continued after Adam's death until 1827, when Playfair's designs were finally expedited, including his magnificent upper library, one of Scotland's most impressive spaces. The new buildings were commissioned during the time that William Robertson was principal of the university. In his thirty years at the helm Robertson worked tirelessly to make Edinburgh one of the leading universities in the world. He was a brilliant historian, a leading figure in the Scottish Enlightenment, an ordained minister, and, among many important positions, moderator of the general assembly of the Church of Scotland. On the page facing, the view from Nicolson Street shows Adam's entrance front, with its Doric columns, which Pevsner describes as 'awe-inspiring . . . nothing is grander in Scotland'.

78 | NICOLSON STREET FROM OLD COLLEGE, 1900. The hustle and bustle of city life is captured in this scene, taken from the perfect vantage point of the old college: as well as pedestrians, there is a vigilant bobby on the beat (*far right*). It may have been a warm day given the number of windows that are open, with residents watching the world go by from their windows.

79 | SURGEONS' HALL, NICOLSON STREET, 1904. Another marvellous William Playfair building, of 1832, with Greek-style portico. It is home to the Royal College of Surgeons of Edinburgh, an august body that was first given official recognition in 1505. There is an interesting museum of surgery within. This photograph by George Washington Wilson is so clear that it captures the man pushing the handcart smoking a pipe!

SURGEON'S HALL & UNIVERSITY BUILDINGS, EDINBURGH. 10,250. G.W.W.

80 | BRISTO STREET, 1900. The name of this much redeveloped street was recorded from 1502 onwards, where it is given as both Birsto and Bristo. According to Stuart Harris – author of the definitive book on the city's place names – there are several shades of meaning but Bristo is perhaps best translated as 'herding place', as this would have been a convenient place in which to herd cattle outside of the old burgh.

81 | MCEWAN HALL, TEVIOT PLACE, c.1900. Sir William McEwan was MP for central Edinburgh in the Liberal interest, an art connoisseur and a noted philanthropist. After working in his uncle's brewery McEwan opened his own brewery, in Fountainbridge, in 1856. The business prospered throughout the British Empire (hence McEwan's Export beer), making him, in the words of a biographer, 'one of Scotland's merchant princes'. He donated £115,000 to build a hall for Edinburgh University, which took his name, and was completed in 1897, at which point he was granted the freedom of the city. It has been used in a variety of ways, but particularly for examinations, graduation ceremonies and concerts.

82 | TEVIOT PLACE/
LAURISTON PLACE, 1900. A
group of children at play outside
the university's medical building.
What they were doing there we
cannot know for certain but
judging by their clothing, which
appears formal, they may have
been on a break from a local
school. The medical faculty was
designed by Sir Robert Rowand
Anderson.

83 | SIR WALTER SCOTT'S
HOUSE, 25 GEORGE
SQUARE, 1905. George Square
was the first major residential
square outside of the Old Town
and was designed and developed
by James Brown in the 1760s. It
became an intellectual hothouse
(think London's Bloomsbury)
and invitations to dine there were
highly prized. The Scott family
moved here from College Wynd
in 1774 when the great novelist
was aged three and he would live
here until he married in 1797.
There is a small plaque on the
wall indicating that Scott resided
here.

THE ROYAL INFIRMARY, EDINBURGH 3113. G.W.W.

THE ROYAL INFIRMARY, EDINBURGH 3113. G.W.W.

84 | ROYAL INFIRMARY OF EDINBURGH FROM THE MEADOWS, early 1900s. Some of the detailing in David Bryce's flamboyant, almost extravagant, infirmary was adumbrated in the building that is his undoubted masterpiece: Fettes college (*see* 98). The Meadows also has an interesting history. Until the eighteenth century it was a loch, before being drained and turned into a park. Such was the general affection for this green lung that an Act of Parliament in 1827 prevented the Meadows from being built upon and today it plays host to all kinds of social and sporting events, although it is no longer used to graze sheep!

AROUND EDINBURGH

There is much more to Edinburgh than the Old and New Towns, with fine architecture to be found outside of these admittedly world-famous areas. The later Victorian and Edwardian periods witnessed further significant expansion as a plethora of residential suburbs appeared. These new developments saw the construction of splendid Victorian terraces in Dean village, outstanding public buildings like Donaldson's hospital and Fettes college in West Coates and East Fettes Avenue respectively, fine residential properties in Bruntsfield and Morningside. There is also one of Scotland's most impressive mediaeval fortresses, Craigmillar castle.

The city has close links to the sea. Leith has traded with the rest of Scotland, England and Europe for centuries, and for much of its history was the busiest port in the country. Newhaven, two miles north of the city centre, was also an important maritime centre, once renowned as a naval dockyard and later as a thriving fishing village. A different type of marine economy took root in Portobello as this handsome coastal suburb became a thriving seaside resort, reaching a peak of popularity in the late nineteenth century.

The photograph on this page (**85**) marks the grand opening of Corstorphine golf club in 1902. This was a nine-hole course, with clubhouse, on the south-western side of Corstorphine hill, and serviced by Pinkhill railway station. Although it was considered to be a fine course with 'bracing air and beautiful views of the surrounding countryside' it disappeared in the 1920s and much of the ground is now occupied by Edinburgh zoo.

◀ **86** | ARTHUR'S SEAT AND SALISBURY CRAGS, 1878. In the heart of Holyrood park's 640 acres, Arthur's Seat (*background, centre*) rises majestically to a peak of 823 feet (251 metres). Formed by an extinct volcano, and often compared to a crouching lion, it is flanked by the jagged edges of Salisbury Crags. There is much of interest here, including an ancient hill fort and the remains of the fifteenth century St Anthony's chapel. It also affords a spectacular views of the city for those energetic enough to climb to the summit.

▲ **87** | EDINBURGH FROM ARTHUR'S SEAT, 1910. A wonderful panorama of Edwardian Edinburgh, with Holyrood palace and abbey on the edge of the park (*right*). The Nelson and Scottish national monuments on Calton hill are clearly visible (*background, centre*) as are the Royal High School of Edinburgh and Calton jail to their left. It is clear there was still a good deal of manufacturing activity in the city, judging by the presence of several large chimneys.

88 | JAMES GILLESPIE'S SCHOOL, 1880 (*this page*). Born in Roslin, James Gillespie (1726–97) became a successful Edinburgh tobacconist with a shop at 231 High Street. He later built a snuff mill in Colinton and these profitable ventures enabled him to acquire several landed estates. When he died he left close to £50,000 to endow a hospital for the elderly and a boys' school.

89 | LOTHIAN ROAD FEATURING ST CUTHBERT'S CHURCH, 1882 (*opp. page*). A highly atmospheric image of Lothian Road in the snow, with horse-drawn carriages and elegantly dressed pedestrians. There has been a St Cuthbert's church on the site since the twelfth century, with many modifications made through the years.

90 | LOTHIAN ROAD: SITE OF USHER HALL. Brewer Andrew Usher donated £100,000 in 1896 for a new concert hall and after much debate this spot was chosen, with the buildings on the right demolished to make way for this important cultural asset. The Usher hall – which because of the tight site sits at an angle to Lothian Road – was designed by J. Stockdale Harrison and completed in 1914.

91 | MORNINGSIDE STATION, MORNINGSIDE ROAD, early 1900s. The station opened in 1884 as part of the South Sub and the following year became part of North British railway company. It was closed to passengers in 1962, and, although the line survives, it is used only for freight trains and the occasional diversion of passenger services.

▲ **92** | UNION CANAL, 1900. Built so that Edinburgh could benefit from cheap coal supplies from the west of Scotland, the Union canal opened in 1822, providing a direct link to the Forth and Clyde canal and hence to Glasgow. With its three major aqueducts and a staircase of eleven locks where it met the Forth and Clyde, this was a major engineering feat. At first the Union flourished but with the development of the railway between the country's two biggest cities its commercial value declined. The original Edinburgh terminal was at Port Hopetoun, at the junction between Lothian Road and Fountainbridge.

▶ **93** | CASTLE TERRACE, c.1900. Not a landmark building but an evocative scene nevertheless with coachmen, horses and spectators, including one lady gazing out from her window. The Castle Terrace bars are long gone.

VIEW FROM DEAN BRIDGE, EDINBURGH. 186.J.V.

◀ **94** | DEAN, c.1900. The Dean estate in the north-west of the city was developed by John Learmonth (1789–1858) a prominent businessman and lord provost of Edinburgh. To improve access to his newly acquired land he engaged the great Scottish engineer, Thomas Telford, to construct a bridge over the Water of Leith, work on which was completed in 1832. The striking church in the centre is Holy Trinity, completed in 1838 to plans by John Henderson as an Episcopalian place of worship. It was in use as an electricity sub-station for several decades but recently reopened as a church.

▲ **95** | VIEW FROM DEAN BRIDGE, n. d. The bridge is required to span a deep gorge and was therefore difficult to design and execute. However, Telford's last major commission – he was by then in his seventies – is one of his finest achievements, his solution to the problem being four spectacular arches rising 106 feet above water level. The bridge provides a dramatic entrance into the city and stunning views over the valley below. The Roman temple-like structure (*right*) is St Bernard's well, designed by the eminent Scottish painter Alexander Nasmyth in 1789.

◀ **96** | BELGRAVE CRESCENT, 1874. A fine Victorian terrace by John Chesser, with two-storey bays and parapets with balustrades. The outlook is spacious and there are attractive gardens, laid out by James Jeffrey in 1876.

▲ **97** | DONALDSON'S SCHOOL FOR THE DEAF, WEST COATES, 1880. Designed by William Playfair, and completed in 1851, this Jacobean-style palazzo is one of the most striking buildings in Edinburgh. It was paid for by a bequest of £215,000 in the will of James Donaldson (1751–1830), a bookseller, owner and editor of the *Edinburgh Advertiser* and a shrewd investor in a range of businesses. Opened by Queen Victoria it is said she was so impressed that she suggested swapping it for Holyrood palace. No longer in use as a school, it is to be redeveloped as luxury apartments.

FETTES COLLEGE, EDINBURGH. 2456 G.W.W.

▲ **98 |** FETTES COLLEGE, EAST FETTES AVENUE, 1904. Sometimes referred to as the 'Eton of Scotland', Fettes has an impressive former-pupil roster that includes judges, aristocrats, generals, cabinet ministers, a prime minister (Tony Blair) and Oscar-winning actress Tilda Swinton. The school was paid for by a legacy of £166,000 in the will of Sir William Fettes, a businessman with interests in many enterprises, most notably in the importation of tea and wine and in banking. The French Gothic design – built on the estate owned by Sir William – is considered by many critics to be architect David Bryce's masterpiece and was completed in 1870.

▶ **99 |** LEITH WALK AND LEITH CENTRAL STATION, 1912. So-called because wheeled traffic was once prohibited, Leith Walk has, since the 1760s, been the principal vehicular link between the city and Leith. One historian notes that by the end of the eighteenth century around a hundred and fifty coaches plied their trade on the route and it is still as busy today. Here we see the 'foot of the Walk' with a tram going past the former Leith central station.

VIEW IN LEITH DOCKS. 4568. G.W.W.

VIEW IN LEITH DOCKS. 294. G.W.W.

100 & 101 | LEITH DOCKS. There has been a settlement in Leith since prehistoric times and it has always been one of Scotland's most important commercial centres. Given its location, the town, inevitably, looked to the sea to make a living and thanks largely to trade with France, the Low Countries and the Baltic states it was Scotland's principal port until the middle of the nineteenth century. This is a point well illustrated by a photograph of 1877 (*opp. page*) of the crowded docks. Leith was also a proud independent burgh until 1920, when, to the dismay of many of its citizens, it was subsumed by Edinburgh. The sailor's home, on this page, (*centre, left*) was designed to accommodate fifty-six seamen, nine officers and fifty shipwrecked sailors in a degree of comfort that was rare for the time. It was built in 1885 and is now a hotel.

102 | ARCHER MEMORIAL FOUNTAIN, LEITH, 1895 (*top left*). The Archers were prominent in both Leith and Trinity and it is a distinct possibility that this memorial honours that family. Sir Gilbert Archer (1882–1948) was a well-known local merchant and both his father and grandfather held the position of registrar in Leith.

103 | MARY OF GUISE'S HOUSE, COAL HILL, 1895 (*bottom left*). Mary of Guise (1515–60) was a French noblewoman who married James V of Scotland in 1538, giving birth to their daughter, the future Mary Queen of Scots, in 1542. After the death of her husband Mary did her best to keep Scotland as a Catholic country, provoking a war with the Protestant nobles, who besieged her forces in Leith.

104 | EASTER ROAD, 1909 (*bottom right*). Until the late eighteenth century Easter (or eastern) Road was the route taken by most coaches travelling from Edinburgh to Leith. The area, which is dominated by tenement housing, has traditionally been the most densely populated in the city, home to waves of newcomers looking for reasonably priced accommodation. The name Easter Road, however, has become almost synonymous with the stadium occupied by Hibernian FC, one of the capital's two great football clubs.

Easter Road.

105 | DUKE STREET, LEITH, 1879 (*top right*). The duke in question is Charles Montagu-Scott, Earl of Dalkeith (1772–1819), who became 4th Duke of Buccleuch and 6th Duke of Queensberry in 1812. An excellent amateur cricketer he was also keen on golf and it is said that he rented a house here to be close to the course on Leith Links.

106 | PORTOBELLO HIGH STREET, 1909 (*bottom left*). A busy day in Portobello with trams, a cyclist, carriages, a cart and people walking on the cobbled street. The tram is advertising Bird's custard while the Central bar is flying the Union Jack.

107 | NEWHAVEN, 1895 (*bottom right*). In this marvellous image by Alexander Inglis, the boats moored on the shore of the Forth (*background*) are evidence of Newhaven's proud maritime traditions. Newhaven, as well as being a thriving fishing village, was also a significant naval dockyard: James IV's giant warship *The Great Michael* was built here in the early sixteenth century. The houses with their sideways' external stairs are also of interest.

108 | CRAIGMILLAR CASTLE, 1880. Built in the fourteenth century – but later expanded – Craigmillar castle is one of Scotland's most impressive mediaeval ruins. The core is the large, L-plan tower house, one of the first of this type ever built, with towering battlements and three-metre-thick walls. Inside there is a warren of rooms, including a fine great hall on the first floor. There is also a Queen Mary's room, where Mary, Queen of Scots is reputed to have slept on her visits to Craigmillar. Indeed, Mary fled here after the 1566 murder of her secretary, David Rizzio.

During the course of the nineteenth century, Edinburgh's population grew rapidly, with commuting became a daily fact of life. While horse buses were available for the better off, many people employed in manual occupations were faced with a long walk to work. There was a need for more efficient transport and so, in 1871, the first horse-drawn trams appeared. The cable tram was introduced in 1888, until it, in turn, was superseded by the electric tram (**109** *below*). The tram was supplemented by the motorised omnibus and as early as 1899 a Daimler wagonette operated on a route between Waterloo Place and Haymarket. In 1905 Scottish Motor Traction, SMT, started a service between the Mound and Corstorphine.

Trains were also important. Waverley station opened in 1846, while the rival Princes Street station came on the scene in the 1890s. An even grander project saw the building of the Forth rail bridge, one of the engineering wonders of the age, and first traversed by train in 1890.

HORSE POWER.

These images show some of the very different uses horses were put to in Victorian Edinburgh. **110** | It is likely that the two horses pulling this Leith-to-Blackford-hill tram sometime in the 1870s (*top left*) would have required the assistance of trace horses along the route. **111** | The packed horse bus to Corstorphine, pictured probably in the 1880s, (*bottom left*) had the benefit of three horses. **112** | The railway bus from Levenhall (*bottom right*), seen here in 1885, was operated by the North British company and would therefore most likely have been heading for Waverley station. **113** | Communities further from the centre of Edinburgh – like Davidson's Mains to the north-west (*opp. page*) – would also have been reliant on the horse to get around, as this image from 1900 illustrates.

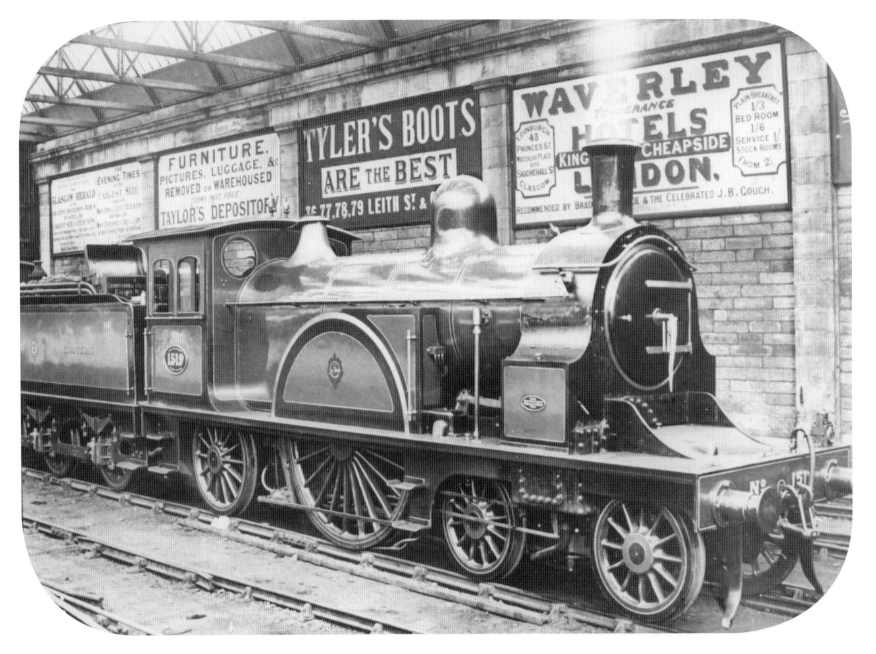

▲ **114** | WAVERLEY STATION, 1900. Between the Old and New towns sits Waverley. Construction began in 1844 but there have been many developments of lines and buildings since then. Covering an area of twenty-five acres it is the largest mainline station in Britain, London excepted, and handles thirty-thousand passengers a day.

▶ **115** | PRINCES STREET STATION, 1900. Built in the 1890s for the Caledonian Railway Company, the Caley, as it was known, was Scotland's biggest station, with seven platforms, a colossal 850-foot-long roof and a site that extended all the way from Rutland Street to Festival Square. It also had the distinct convenience of being accessible from street level. The station thrived until the late 1940s and was the destination of choice for the royal family on their visits to the capital. Sadly, due to rationalisation, it was closed in 1965. As both photographs show, this was very much the age of steam.

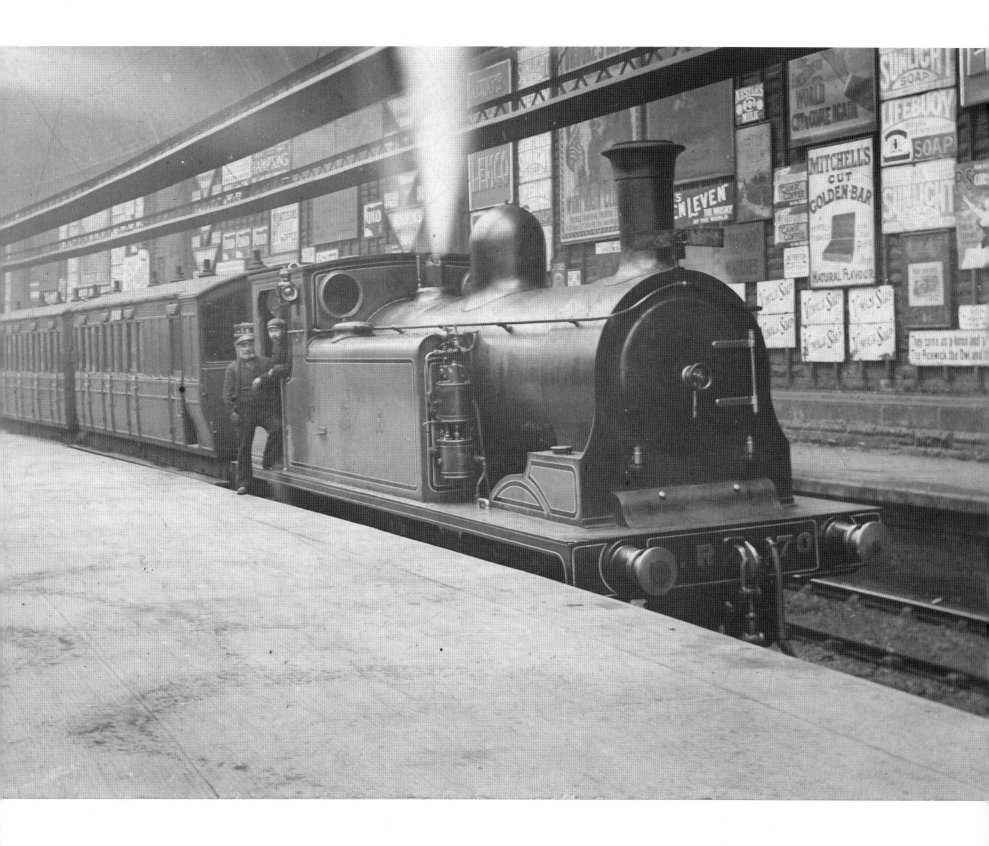

116 | MR BINKO'S ELECTRIC RAILWAY, 1884 (*top left*). William Ewart Gladstone, himself of Scottish heritage, was prime minister four times in the second half of the nineteenth century. He is pictured here peering out of a carriage on Mr Binko's electric railway, exhibited by Henry Binko at the international forestry exhibition, which was held in the grounds of Donaldson's school.

117 | OPENING OF BARNTON RAILWAY STATION, 1894 (*bottom left*). Originally known as Cramond Brig station, the name Barnton was used from 1903. Barnton was part of the Caledonian Railway Company's suburban branch line. It closed to passenger traffic in 1951 although the station buildings stood until the 1980s.

118 | OPENING OF LEITH CENTRAL STATION, 1903 (*bottom right*). This impressive station was built by the North British railway company and passenger trains ran between here and Waverley from 1903 until 1952. It is said that Leith central was the biggest station built from scratch in twentieth century Scotland. As well as the rather unassuming main entrance below the clock tower, the station could also be accessed via a subway entrance on Easter Road and, for vehicles, by a carriageway from Leith Walk. Leith central's main claim to fame is that the best-selling novel and cult film *Trainspotting*, by Irvine Welsh, takes its name from the station.

OPENING OF BARNTON RAILWAY
SPEECH BY SIR JAMES MAITLAND BART

THE OPENING OF LEITH CENTRAL STATION

119 | THE CABBIE, 1900 (*top right*). At the corner of Newington Road and Salisbury Place a cabbie – or perhaps the dispatcher – touts for customers. His colleague, meanwhile, keeps a firm grip on the taxi's horse.

120 | FIRE BRIGADE ON CALL, 1913 (*bottom left*). Galloping horses and fire engines on crowded city streets were a thrilling sight for bystanders.

121 | BOATING, CRAMOND BRIG, 1895 (*bottom right*). A picturesque scene on the river Almond. In the background is the old Cramond brig, which dates from the fifteenth century and anciently marked the boundary between Edinburghshire and Linlithgowshire. It is said that James V (1512–42) was attacked as he crossed the bridge but was saved by Jock Howieson, a tenant farmer. The King rewarded Howieson by granting him ownership of the land he rented.

122 & 123 | THE FORTH RAIL BRIDGE. Railway companies were keen on a Forth bridge to ensure a continuous east-coast line from London to Aberdeen. Work began in 1883 and the contract was let to the great Scottish engineer, Sir William Arrol. Thanks to Arrol's organisational prowess it took a peak workforce of 4,600 men just six years to span the Queensferry narrows with the Prince of Wales performing the opening ceremony on 4 March 1890. The first major project completed entirely in steel it has three enormous cantilevers, with two 1,700-foot spans suspended between them, at the time the longest spans in the world. The photographs show the bridge under construction (*this page*) and with a steam train crossing in the 1890s (*opp. page*).

FORTH BRIDGE FROM SOUTH. 6971. G.W.W.
HEIGHT 369 FD. LENGTH (INCLUDING VIADUCT) 8098 FD. SPANS 1710 FD EACH.

THE FORTH BRIDGE, FROM SOUTH.   6971.   G.W.W.
HEIGHT, 369ft.; LENGTH, INCLUDING VIADUCT 8098ft., SPANS 1710ft. EACH.

124 | DOUBLE-DECKER BUS, 1906. The Scottish Motor Traction Company Ltd (SMT) acquired its first double-deckers, in 1906, from the Maudslay Motor Company of Coventry. This was the city centre-to-Corstorphine bus, which, as well as the driver and conductor, had a full load of passengers. Journeys for people on the upper deck must have been bracing given the lack of a roof, hence the preponderance of hats, scarves and overcoats.

Edinburgh's People

The final section of this book is devoted to the good citizens of Edinburgh, whether at work, play, shopping or even taking part in political protests. While it has long been one of the most affluent places in Britain many of its people have had to struggle to make a living: the fisher folk of Newhaven, the horse traders who flocked to Grassmarket, men no longer fit to work, the poverty stricken who in the nineteenth century found cheap accommodation on Cowgate and Canongate. They have all played a part in Edinburgh's story.

We are fortunate that the city was home to some of the world's greatest photographic pioneers, men like David Octavius Hill (1802–70). An established artist and secretary to the Royal Scottish Academy, Hill famously began a collaboration with photographer Robert Adamson in 1843. Adamson had established a studio at Rock house, where he attempted to perfect the calotype photograph.

Together Hill, the artist, and Adamson, the technician, were responsible for a memorable collection of photographs, ranging from individual portraits to groups. Quite astonishingly for the time they produced close to two thousand pictures in just over four years. One of their greatest achievements was to capture the hardy souls who sailed out from the village of Newhaven in search of herring. These and many of their other seminal works are on display in the National Portrait Gallery in Queen Street and they show why Hill and Adamson are so highly regarded in the history of photography.

125 | DAVID OCTAVIUS HILL, 1847.

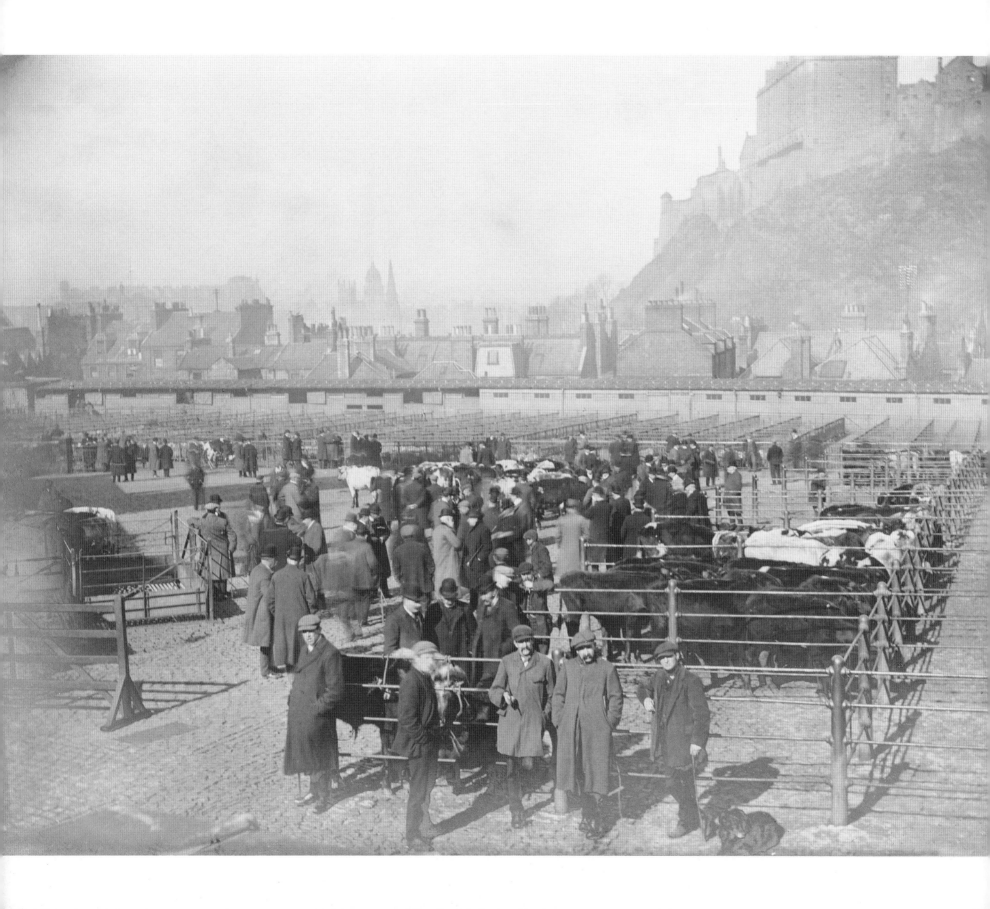

126 & 127 | MARKETS. Until the nineteenth century the Old Town hosted a range of markets, selling everything from fish, poultry and corn to farm animals, including pigs, sheep, cattle and horses. There was even a slaughterhouse under North Bridge. The Grassmarket was one of the busiest sites for livestock sales but when the council bought land in Lauriston Place the cattle and sheep market moved in 1844 (*opp. page*) and stayed there until 1911, when purpose-built premises were built in Gorgie. The horse market did not initially move to Lauriston Place but continued to be held in Grassmarket (*this page*) when it too made the move in 1911 to Gorgie.

128 | INDIAN TROOPS ON PRINCES STREET, c.1900. Big crowds turned out for this military parade. It is striking how well-dressed the spectators were, with the fine millinery – including bowlers, top hats, flat caps, bonnets, and, of course, turbans – a particular feature.

129 | SUFFRAGETTE DEMONSTRATION, PRINCES STREET, 1909. Women had been campaigning for the vote since 1866 but by the Edwardian period matters had taken on a more militant stance, which in its turn provoked a violent backlash from the police. Women from Edinburgh were prominent in the movement and this photograph shows the huge numbers of campaigners who marched along Princes Street on 8 October 1909 in what became known as the great procession and women's demonstration. Despite the best efforts of the suffragettes it would not be until 1918 that women were granted the vote, and even then it was only those over the age of thirty who qualified.

130 | NEWHAVEN FISHERMEN, 1847 (*top left*). A vivid photograph by David Octavius Hill and colleague Robert Adamson, one of a series they took of the fisher-folk of Newhaven. Although the photo is un-posed Hill and Adamson carefully delineated the eleven men, such that all of their heads are in clear view.

131 | CITADEL ARCH, DOCK STREET, LEITH, c.1912 (*top right*). In the 1650s, as part of Oliver Cromwell's policy to tighten his grip on Scotland, a number of citadels were built, including in Leith, which, with its bustling port, was strategically significant. The arch shown here was one of the gates, or ports, into the citadel. While the house above has now been demolished, the arch is extant.

132 | CHILDREN OF COWGATE, early 1900s (*bottom right*). Once home to the aristocracy and Scotland's wealthy elite, by the nineteenth century Cowgate had many slum dwellings and had become almost a byword for poverty. The two children on the right are shoeless.

133 | INJURED WORKER, 1885 (*opp. page*). This unfortunate gentleman had been injured in an explosion in Noble's works in Falkirk in 1879, leaving him blind and unfit to follow his former occupation. To make what was no doubt a meagre living he had been reduced to selling matches on the streets of Edinburgh.

PORTOBELLO PIER.   10,563.   G.W.W.

134 | PORTOBELLO PIER, 1904. 'Porty', as it was known to locals, was a thriving beach resort well into the twentieth century and even today attracts crowds of bathers when the sun is shining. This grand pier was built in 1871 at a cost of £10,000 and stretched over the sands and into the Firth of Forth. At the end of the pier there was a pierrot theatre, and holidaymakers could also catch a ferry for a day trip on the Forth. It was dismantled in 1917 after being badly damaged in a storm.

135 | SCOTTISH NATIONAL EXHIBITION, SAUGHTON PARK, 1908. The exhibition ran for six months, between May and October 1908, attracting 3.5 million paying customers. It was inspired by a very successful previous exhibition, on the Meadows, in 1886. However, as the Meadows were not available, the city council granted organisers the use of forty-three acres at Saughton park. A railway station was specially created for visitors, who were able to enjoy a wide range of attractions. As well as halls devoted to industry, with exhibits from across the globe, there was a music hall, a fine-art gallery, restaurants and a large amusement park, complete with water chute.

Acknowledgements

First published in 2016 by Fort Publishing Ltd, Old Belmont House, 12 Robsland Avenue, Ayr, KA7 2RW

© James McCarroll, 2016

James McCarroll has asserted his rights under the Design, Patents and Copyright Act, 1988 to be identified as the author of this work. No part of this publication may be reproduced without the permission of the publishers.

Photographs courtesy of:

Historic Environment Scotland (HES): Title page (right), Contents page, 5, 20, 32, 36, 40, 43, 48, 66, 68, 86, 93, 127. HES/Scottish Colorfoto Collection: 2, 6, 9, 10, 15, 18, 32, 54, 57, 64, 72, 76, 81, 87, 88, 97. HES/Chrystal Collection: 11, 16, 22, 33, 34, 35, 37, 39, 73, 75, 77, 78, 80, 92, 94, 96, 99, 135. HES/Francis M. Chrystal Collection: 113, 131. HES/Bedford Lemere: 49, 59, 71. HES/William Notman Collection: 23, 61, 101. HES/Thomas Polson Lugton: 41. HES/Whytock and Reid Collection: 108. Crown Copyright/HES/Edinburgh Photographic Society Collection: 126. HES/George Washington Wilson photograph: 12

SCRAN/National Museums Scotland: 8, 83, 85, 104, 109, 110, 115. SCRAN/Royal Commission on the Ancient and Historical Monuments of Scotland: 38, 67, 69, 91, 118, 132. SCRAN/Edinburgh City Libraries: 38. SCRAN/Dundee City Libraries: 52. SCRAN/St Andrew's University Library: 62. SCRAN/Scottish Motor Museum Trust: 124. SCRAN/Glencoe and North Lorn Folk Museum: 114. SCRAN/Scottish Life Archive, National Museums of Scotland: 111.

University of Aberdeen/George Washington Wilson collection: Front cover, back cover, 1, 3, 7, 13, 14, 19, 27, 42, 45, 55, 56, 58, 60, 70, 74, 79, 84, 98, 100, 122, 123, 134

Scottish National Portrait Gallery: *24, **25, *26, *28, *29, **30, **31, *44, **51, **89, **90, *95, **116, 128
(*Gift of Mrs Riddell in memory of Peter Fletcher Riddell, 1985; **Edinburgh Photographic Society Collection, gifted 1897)

Capital Collections/Edinburgh City Council: Title page (left), 50, 102, 103, 105, 106, 107, 112, 117, 119, 121, 125, 130

Copyright The Francis Frith Collection: 46, 53, 63, 65

Getty Images: 4, 17, 21, 47, 82, 133

Mirrorpix: 129

Scottish Fire and Rescue: 120

Typeset by 3btype.com

Graphic design of cover by Mark Blackadder

Front-cover and chapter-heading titles by Doreen Shaw

Thanks also to Anne Lyden, SNPG; Clare Padgett, Edinburgh City Council; Kim Downie, University of Aberdeen; Neil Fraser, Canmore; Julia Skinner, Francis Frith Collection; Dave Farries, Scottish Fire and Rescue Service.

Printed and bound in China by 1010 Printing International Ltd

ISBN: 978-1-905769-51-3